My papery package
will split open
and I'll wriggle out
into the sunshine!
When my wings are
dry, I'll fly around
and drink nectar
from flowers.

A BUTTERFLY!

1. When I'm ready, I'll lay my tiny eggs on a leaf.

2. They'll hatch into little caterpillars that will eat and grow . . .

**3.** until they are MUCH bigger.

**4.** Then they'll each make a small papery package and hang under a leaf by a silken thread . . .

ready to become a butterfly!

I'm newly born, pink and white and blind. I'm so small that you could hold me in one hand.

WHAT WILL I BE?

**1.** I'll go seal hunting with my mom on the frozen sea. When I'm older, I'll hunt seals on my own.

**2.** I'll grow and grow until my feet are as big as dinner plates!

3. Then, one winter, I'll make a den under the snow.

4. And have pink and white babies of my own!

I'm round and white, like a Ping-Pong ball. I lie underneath warm sand.

WHAT WILL I BE?

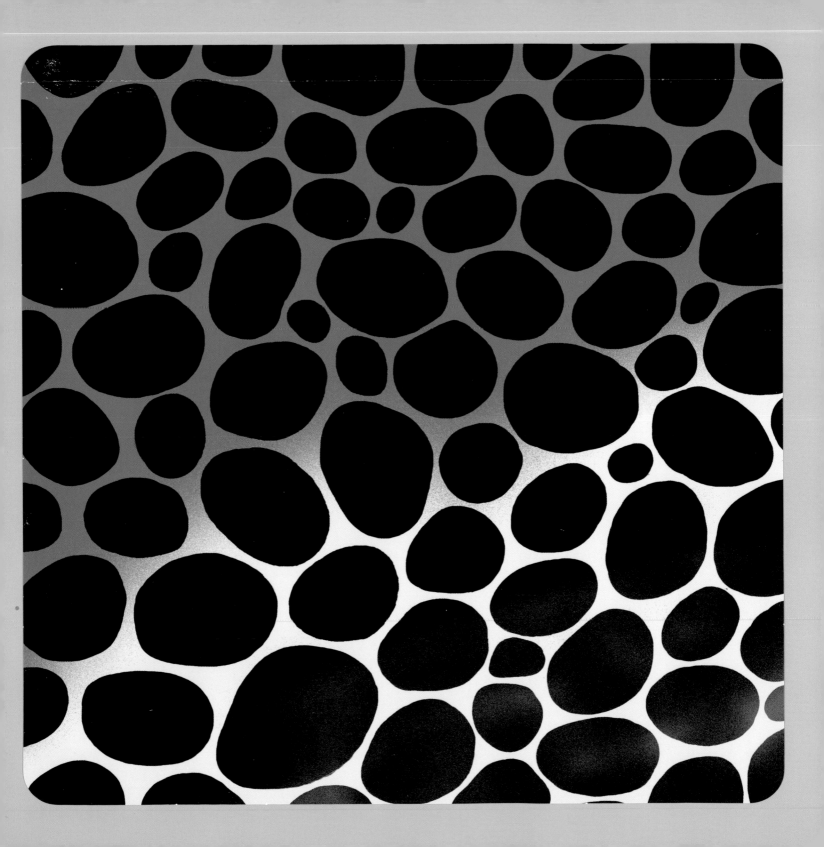

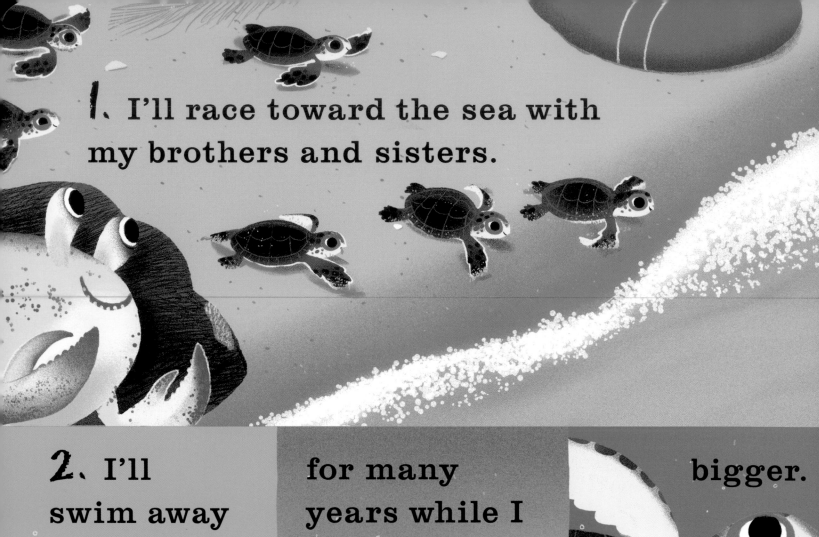

**1.** I'll race toward the sea with my brothers and sisters.

**2.** I'll swim away and wander the sea . . .

for many years while I grow . . .

bigger.

**3.** When I'm very big, I'll come back to the beach where I was born.

**4.** I'll lay eggs, round and white like Ping-Pong balls, in the warm sand.

I'm a black dot in a blob
of jelly, floating in a pond.

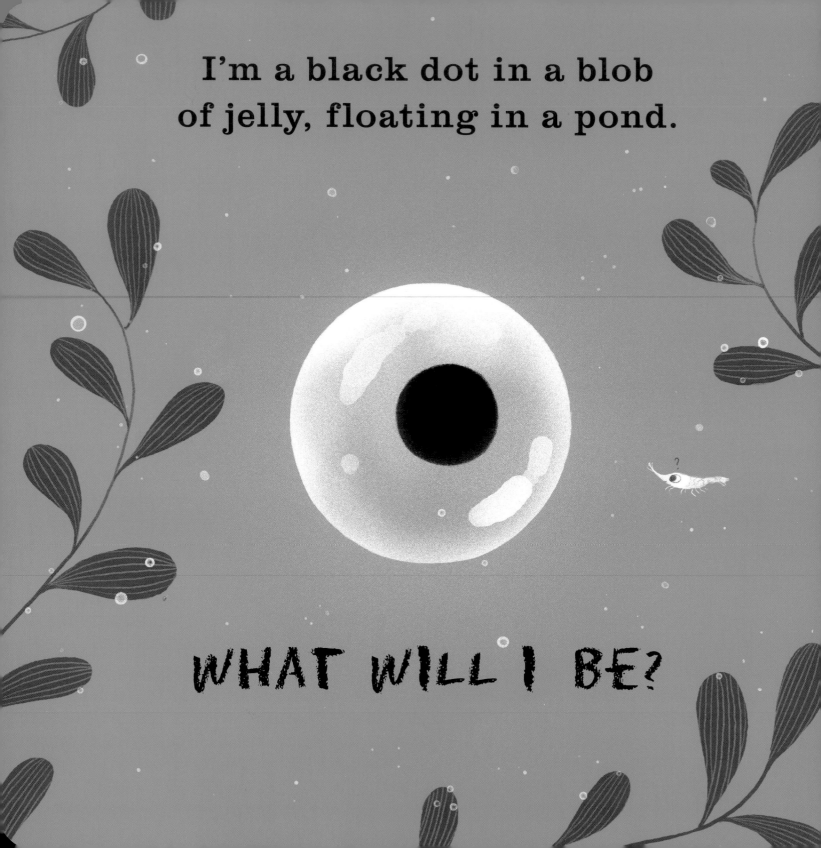

WHAT WILL I BE?

**1.** I'll swim around the pond and grow front legs.

**2.** Then I'll grow back ones.

**3.** I'll lose my tail and turn into a teeny frog and hop away.

**4.** When I've grown much, MUCH **bigger,** I'll come back to the pond to lay lots of eggs that look like dots in blobs of jelly.

I'm smooth and speckled
and smaller than a grape.

WHAT WILL I BE?

1. My eyes will open.

2. Then my feathers will sprout.

**3.** Soon I'll flap my wings and fly away.

**4.** And next year I'll make a nest for my own smooth, speckled eggs.

What will they be?
Match the colors
to find out.

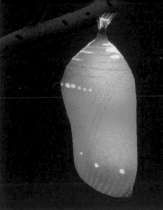

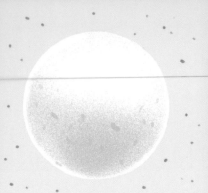
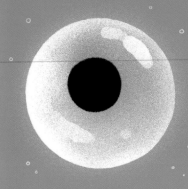